WARNING

This book is not for women

This book is for a man who wants to master how to be confident through mastering strong eye contact like a fearless alpha male.

If you want the bad boys/real men's dirty truth about how to use eye contact to develop your confidence as a man—which will help you in relationship, getting women attracted to you and in public speaking, then this is for you.

Only a few men know what you're about to discover, so count yourself lucky and get ready.

DEDICATION

I dedicate this book to all the women who rejected me, blocked me on social media, and broke my heart for being a nice guy. You forced me to become a bad boy and a man. Here I am to share all I know about women, great sex, and relationship secrets.

INTRODUCTION

☙❧

This book will turn you from that shy guy who rarely makes eye contact to the Swift who makes elders nervous by looking them straight in the eye until they become the first to look away.

Confidence is a sexy skill and clothes to wear. A man with it is a man with a brighter future. To some, confidence is natural, but to most, it must be learned.

The easiest way to develop your confidence is by mastering the **Eyes** and putting yourself in the real world. This book can be finished in few minutes.

It has the only secret you need to develop a magnetic personality with your eyes alone. When you look someone dead in the eye, you'll appear confident in the receiver's eyes.

He or she will become shy, nervous, or will be wondering what is going on. Now, adding a smile or a wink will ease them into knowing you're flirting with their brains.

What else is sexier than a confident man or woman? Even Mark Twain was always nervous just like most people. When giving a speech, he couldn't look people in the eye too.

He learned it the hard way, but here, we are to make things easy for you. If someone had introduced this to him, it would have been an easy road.

You're at luck to have this secret in the open. At the end of this three-chapter book, you'll learn **Intense Eye**

Contact, **Magnetic Left Eye Wink,** and **The Blurry Eye** to set you apart from the rest of the men and women of this world.

By this time tomorrow or next week, you'll testify the same good testimony as Mr. Swift did in this book. He testified how powerful this system is.

How he does it to elderly ones everywhere he goes. Put a smile on your face as you read and practice this simple trick. In fact, it's not a trick, but a life and confidence building weapon. ALL MEN MUST KNOW THIS.

TABLE OF CONTENT

TESTIMONIAL

ಬಿಐ

"I have seen and read the PDF. It's the bomb. Thank you for writing the book. It's an eye-opener for people like us who like to look away when we see women in general." - Evans

"Straight to the point book with amazing tips."

CHAPTER 1

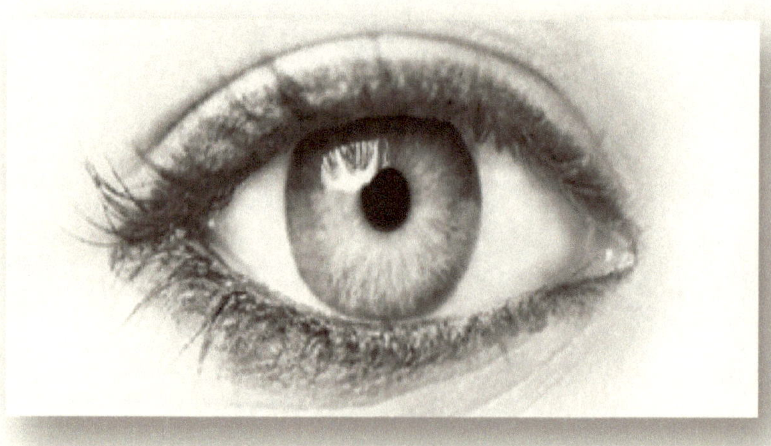

How to Train Your Eyes to Make a Strong Eye Contact and Appear Confident with Women and Men in General

Do you know how powerful the eyes are? Do you know they're the windows to the soul? Do you know your eyes alone can make you appear confident and get you what you want in the dating world and in life in general?

It's sexy, intimidating, and sometimes creepy in a good

way. You will have the power after reading. It's a promise.

What I'm about to say is crazy; some of you will NEVER believe it. When I was learning how to keep eye contact for long, I embarked on a crazy training called the "Triangular Gaze."

I surfed the web for hours looking for the top 5 most beautiful Africans, Asians, Americans, Europeans, and Australians. I looked for a pictures where their eyes were looking straight into the camera like the picture below.

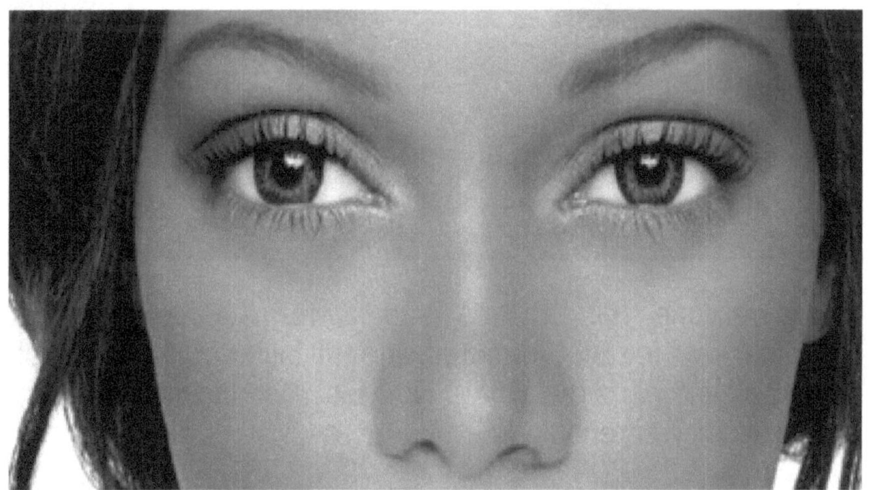

Get a picture of a lady/man you'd be terrified to approach or have sex with on a normal day. A picture you think is too sexy and hot while looking straight at the camera.

Imagine there's an inverted triangle on her face. From her cute left eye (#1) to her cute right eye (#2) to her sexy lips (#3), then back to her number 1 again. With this image in your head, you'll have a triangle on her face.

When facing the picture or girl, pick only one eye; the

eye on your right-hand side, which is her left eye. Act as if nothing else exists on her face but the chosen eye.

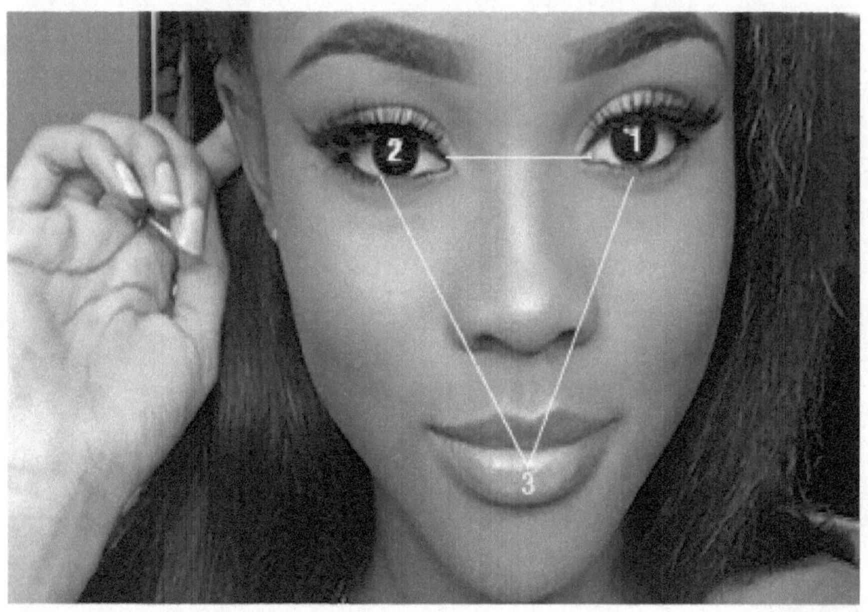

Everyone has an iris and a retina. Look at that particular eye for 5-10 minutes without blinking. Make it look as if that is where the whole world is. Nothing else matters except what you're looking at.

Concentrate on her pupil. The pupil is a tiny black dot at the center of her eyes—it gets bigger during arousal or naughty thoughts, but gets smaller during aggression/fear. In your head, have this mindset of, **"Who the fuck do you think you are?"**

And a little naughty 'smile' on your face while looking at the eye. Don't break your gaze despite the distractions or lust. It'll get to a point tears will start dropping from your eyes, but keep pushing until you reach your mark.

When I started, my first attempt was 45 minutes, and

luckily, I made it an hour without blinking (this is exactly what I said most of you won't believe, but don't worry, it's the truth).

I did mine with a computer and the brightness was at its maximum. I shed tears like rain, but it was worth it. Now, the only person I break eye contact with is an angry soldier. Everyone else bows before me in eye contact contest.

To me, it's like a competition of who's going to look away first, and it must be you, because I'm already trained for it.

When you're done with the eye, you take a break and wipe your tears (by then, your eyes would be reddish). Now, it's time to do the same with the other eye. When you're done, you should do the same with her lips.

While confidently looking at her lips, you should say in your mind, **"You think your lips are sexy, huh? No, they ain't."** Have this mentality of: "They aren't sexy," even when you know they are, but while disagreeing with her in your head, slowly bring in a naughty smile. These disagreements in your head is a technique to avoid being too lust in the moment.

Note: to do this exercise better, use your phone with an earpiece and play some songs you love and you'll see how time will fly. To conquer this exercise, do it with different cute woman, men, and older men of high profile.

If you do this exercise for a week or two, your confidence will increase. And when you make eye contact with people who look less attractive or powerful than those you've practiced with, it'll make you care less on the outcome.

Men who can't last longer is bed is not because they can't, but because their PC muscles aren't developed. If they develop them (as taught in book 7) they'll permanently cure their PEs and last as long as they want in bed. So, in life and in dating, those who care less, get the ball. This same thing applies to sex.

When you make that eye contact, the other person will be the first to look away, because yours will be fierce and it'll exude confidence and it's a little intimidating. Don't you EVER look away first, except the person is a dangerous terrorist.

If the person looks away before you, and you're sure you've made a strong eye contact, don't look her way again, but use your peripheral vision to monitor her, because she'll definitely try to look back.

In her head, she'll be wondering what kind of a man is this. And she'd want to know you. (If she hasn't yet.) It's psychological. It's irresistible. Women can't explain it and they can't control it.

Some years ago, I was at the bank and I sighted a cute girl. I was unkempt, but trendy. I looked like a rugged bad boy. I saw her and acted as if I didn't notice her, but I was using my peripheral vision to monitor her when she'll look my way, because I was the only young guy on the queue filled with old pensioners.

My cap is really an attention grabber, so she tried to steal a glance, but I caught her and glued my eyes with hers. She wanted to act tough and keep the eye contact until I look away, but she was messing with the wrong guy. After some seconds, she bowed and focused her attention somewhere else.

I also focused mine somewhere else, but was using my

peripheral vision to monitor her. Damn! This girl was always staring, thinking I didn't see her. When she was done, she disappeared from her queue and reappeared on my right-hand side.

I turned and saw her big ass and breast standing beside me doing nothing and looking all nervous. I was shocked. I ignored her. After 20 seconds, she went upstairs and immediately came down, then exited the bank.

While waiting on the queue for my turn, she came back and headed upstairs again. Her ass and her boobs were too big for her age. Then, I said enough is enough and deed the needful.

She was nervous, but happy at the same time. I looked so rough and dangerous. So, I understand her nervousness. Some women love dangers.

Some people are natural eye contact makers and keepers. If you're one of them, congratulations, but if you aren't, please spare some time from your busy schedule and learn a new skill—you'll never regret it, I promise.

CHAPTER 2

You need to also master how to wink at humans in general. Winking at girls should be a bonus mark. For me, I wink at guys if I don't want to greet them verbally. It makes life easier.

Winking has some emotional charges and it is triggered more on the receivers of the wink. The wink will not make sense to (you) the winker, but the "winkee" if such a word exists.

I learned this thing from a guy. He uses body language

to talk most times. If you see him, you'll think he's a snob or gay, because he uses body language a lot.

The first day he did it to me, I was shocked. I was greeting him verbally, but he didn't reply verbally. Instead, he used his left eye to wink at me. I got the code he sent nonverbally.

I stumbled on a song called Dorobucci on YouTube and see how one of the singers used a similar winking technique and the wink started trending on Twitter. Girls know how winks react in their bodies. It's magical. You don't need to be cute to wink. Any man who doesn't wink is missing.

This is How to Do It:

Keep your face calm as if you're reminiscing the past or thinking about your future. Make a humble and sorry-face as if you're on another planet or as if you've lost somebody and you're helpless or speechless.

This facial outlook will calm all the muscles on your face and you'll appear gentle, relaxed, or calm. That facial look you get when you're about to fall asleep.

Take a look at these girls' calm and sober facial expressions. If they ask you for help with this kind of facial expressions, you'll help them without thinking twice. The calmness or innocence on their faces is the magic.

If they wink at you, you're going to melt. This is exactly
the same thing you should do to women in and outside the

bedroom.

If you master this magnetic (left) eye wink (you can choose your right eye if you wish), you'll attract women or people to like you faster.

To do it, you'll need to induce or hypnotize yourself to get in that state of "calm mind" in seconds. It's instantaneous.

Step by Step:

Imagine you're on another planet: Lonely and forgotten by people on earth. Make a sorry and helplessly calm facial expression.

Do it now! Relax all the stubborn muscles on your face. Did you notice how calm your face is? If somebody sees you now he/she will probably ask you, "What are you thinking about?"

Now, wink your left eye ONLY and keep the right eye wide open. Do this 20-50 times continuously and you'll master it in less than 2 hours.

Applying it on a Girl:

The moment your eyes meet any girl's eyes, magnet hers with your wink. You don't EVER need to approach her, so don't worry about that. It's only called IOI (indicator of interest).

When you meet her 20 years later, she'll think she had met you before and will open up to you more than anyone else who hasn't winked at her the way you did.

The magnetic left eye wink is like being on the queue in

a girl's life, but with the highest or second to the highest rank. A woman will forever remember a guy who used that calm and gentle facial expression to wink at her. It's sexy and romantic to women. THEY LOVE IT.

Use it in the bedroom too and it will emote and immerse her into the moment. It amplifies the feelings and women are suckers for emotional feelings. They can't get enough.

If she's a new girl, the moment your eyes meet **JUST MAGNET HER** and don't worry about approaching if you don't want to. I use this to tease girls every single day and I won't approach most of them, because I'm only teasing and not taking it seriously.

When you do approach some of them, they'll talk as if they had known you for years. The **Magnetic Left Eye Wink** gives a hot, calm, and naughty good-bad boy impression. Women love it.

You don't need to be as cute as Brad Pitt—just make sure you master it. Only wink once at her in a slow-motion kind of way, then ignore her entirely, but use your peripheral vision to catch when she's stealing some glances.

Sometimes, burst into a semi-naughty smile after the wink. It's just a tease. **The INTENSE Eye Contact** and **The Magnetic Left Eye Wink** have lots of benefits and some are.

1. Confidence (she'll think you're confident).
2. Sexy (being confident automatically makes you look sexy).
3. You've created quick rapport in seconds.
4. She'll easily be receptive if you approach her.
5. If you're in the bedroom, she'll be wet by now.

6. She'll think of you throughout the day, etc.

Now, go and practice and you'll see for yourself. The code is: Practice with intensity, but when using it on real women, soften it. Never look away first. It's a woman's job to shy away from a dominant man, then smile at her nervousness as you use your naughty smile to make her comfortably curious.

After mastering this system, you'll develop your rules on how to use it yourself. You'll instinctively know when your eye contact or wink is becoming creepy and when it's sexy. Your instinct will always guide you. You rock!

Test / Exercise 1

Whenever you're watching the news, look straight into the eye of the presenter throughout her duration on screen. Whenever you're watching a movie, sports, or anything on TV, look into the eye of anyone on screen without blinking. This training will help you a lot to be confident.

Test / Exercise 2

Look at her left eye *ONLY* for 5 minutes without being distracted by anything on her body. Then, start a triangular gaze from her left eye (5 minutes) to her right (5 minutes), then to her lips (5 minutes).

It's a 15 minutes exercise. Focus on her pupil if you can see it. Don't blink. You should shed tears with this exercise; else, you're doing it wrongly. Hold yours like a man.

Put on a horny and calm facial expression as you look at her. When it gets to her lips, put a naughty squint on your face as you gaze. At the end of each gaze, wink at her with smiles.

The practice image, but you can download yours.

Let's assume the girl above is a girl you want. When looking at her, use your INTENSE Eye contact to turn her on. As you try the triangular gaze, imagine all the naughty things you'll do to her in the bedroom.

Say them in your head. Be naughty. As you imagine these while looking intensely into her eye (her pupil), whatever you're imagining inside you, will transfer to her.

If you're feeling horny, it will get to her and she'll unconsciously feel the same. This is nonverbal immersion and it works. In the bedroom, end it with a smile and innocently bite your lips as you wink at her. All these are parts of foreplay and they turn women on.

Here is a chat between Covey and Swift

Swift: ...you're right.
Swift: Sometimes I think it's magic.
Swift: And the eye contact thing you taught a while ago is amazing.
Swift: I'll look girls and they'll become shy and remove their eyes.

Covey: Yes. The eye contact lecture is magic. I deleted all of them.
Swift: I still have them in my brain.
Covey: Haha. It's very intimidating. They'll become shy.
Swift: I tend to do it with elders too.

CHAPTER 3

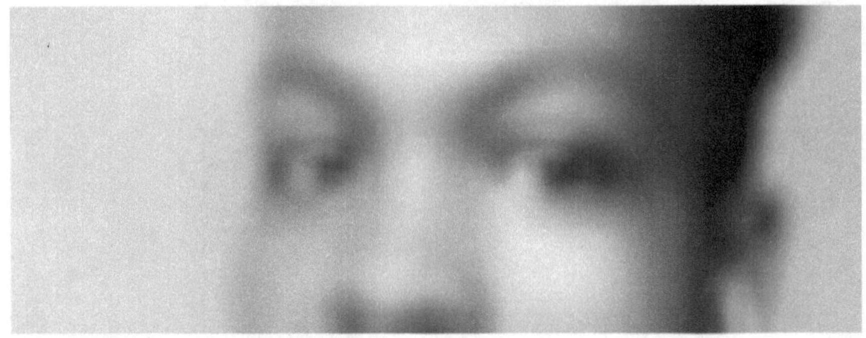

Here is the main secret I refused to reveal—it's called **The Blurry Eye.** At a point in this exercise, you'll look into anyone's eye, but they won't look into yours.

It's the magic. Let me explain the blurry eye. Have you ever had a hazy mood where you're seeing things, but not clearly? Yes, that is the blurry eye.

You can do it on command after mastering this system. This blurry eye is the best. It makes you punish anybody who tries to hold eye contact with you. "Punish how?" you asked.

Okay, listen. When your eyes are locked with someone who has a strong eye contact power just like you, some students may freak out, but the hazy eye is here to save you.

The moment you switch to the hazy eye, it blurs your sight or vision while still looking at your target. You'll keep looking at the person, but you'll be in dreamland while they're suffering looking at you in real life.

The hazy or blurry eye makes you detach yourself from

the eye contact, but you're still making a strong eye contact. It saves you energy.

The other person will be the one suffering while trying to keep the eye contact. At a point, they'll give up. The hazy eye will turn you to someone who has eyes but can't see, yet you're looking, but in a blurry manner.

To practice the blurry eye, put a picture in your front, see it vividly, then begin to blur your eyes until you can't see the picture clearly (pixelated).

Do this 5 to 10 times for 20 minutes. With this, you'll master it in no time. You can also do it with texts on a paper or on screen.

To Do:

Starting from today, any picture of a lady you see, picture an inverted triangle on her face. Look into her left eye. After some seconds, smile, then blur it.

Take this into the real world and do it. Do it to all your friends and relations. You'll be glad you did.

Note: It's good not to look away, but it's also good to know when to look away first. Sometimes, being the first to look away in a relaxed way has power too.

It shows you don't care. Keeping the eye contact shows you care and you're confident. Instinctively choose the one that fits your situation. Don't be a robot—be flexible.

Your confidence will be staggering after using this book. Please, don't abuse this system. Be congenial with it. Thank you.

Bruh..forgot my password 15:08

Could you help me reset it... 15:08

What's your moniker? 15:13

15:36

I have Finally figured it out... 15:36

Alright 19:13

DECEMBER 21, 2017

Seen and read the PDF 16:17

Its the bomb... 16:17

Thanks for writing the book 16:18

Its an eye opener for people like us who like to look away when we see women in general...  16:18